Look at Me!
Self-portraits in art

by Ruth Thomson

An imprint of Hodder Headline Limited

Titles in this series:

Action! Movement in art
Families: Relationships in art
Look At Me! Self-Portraits in art
Place and Space: Landscapes in art
Sculpture: Three dimensions in art
Telling Tales: Stories in art

For more information about this series
and other Hodder Wayland titles, go to
www. hodderwayland.co.uk

Series concept: Ruth Thomson
Series Consultant: Erika Langmuir
Editor and Picture Research: Margot Richardson
Designers: Rachel Hamdi and Holly Mann

Text copyright © Ruth Thomson 2005

British Library Cataloguing in Publication Data
  Thomson, Ruth
  Look at me: self portraits. - (Artventure)
  1.Self-portraits - Juvenile literature 2.Art appreciation -
  Juvenile literature
  I.Title
  704.9'42

ISBN 0 7502 43376

Printed in China

The publishers would like to thank the following for permission
to reproduce their pictures:
Page 1 akg-images, London; 4-5 Printed by permission of the
Norman Rockwell Family Agency, Copyright © 1960 the
Norman Rockwell Family Entities/Transparency courtesy of The
Curtis Publishing Company, Indianapolis, USA; 6 akg-images; 7
© Gianni Dagli Orti/CORBIS; 8-9 © Tate London 2004; 10 ©
Estate of Stanley Spencer 2003. All Rights Reserved,
DACS/Transparency courtesy Fitzwilliam Museum, Cambridge;
11 © Arte & Immagini srl/CORBIS; 12-13 © Francis G.
Mayer/CORBIS; 14 © 2004 Banco de México Diego Rivera &
Frida Kahlo Museums Trust Av. Cinco de Mayo No. 2, Col.
Centro, Del. Cuauhtémoc 06059, México, D.F./Transparency
courtesy Agency Photographique de la Réunion des Musées
Nationaux, Paris © Photo CNAC/MNAM Dist. RMN; 15
Narodni Galerie, Prague, Czech
Republic/www.bridgeman.co.uk; 16-17 © ADAGP, Paris and
DACS, London 2003/Transparency courtesy Stedelijk Museum,
Amsterdam, on loan from the Netherlands Institute for Cultural
Heritage; 18-19 © Peter Blake 2003. All Rights Reserved, DACS/
© Tate, London 2004; 20 © National Gallery Collection; By
kind permission of the Trustees of the National Gallery,
London/CORBIS; 21 © Francis G. Mayer/CORBIS; 23 akg-
images/Erich Lessing; 24 © The Andy Warhol Foundation for the
Visual Arts, Inc./ARS, NY and DACS, London 2003/The Andy
Warhol Museum, Pittsburgh; 25 © Archivi Alinari, Firenze, Italy;
26 © Eduardo Paolozzi 2003. All Rights Reserved, DACS/photo
by Ken Kirkwood.

weblinks

For more information about
self-portraits in art, go to
www.waylinks.co.uk/series/
artventure/selfportraits

Contents

Words in **bold** can be found in the glossary

Making a self-portrait

Self-portraits are works made by artists to show themselves as they wish to be seen. They may show how artists work; their interests, workplace, country, family, or even pets. They can be in any **medium**, such as drawings, paintings, photos, or sculptures.

❑ Norman Rockwell
Triple Self-Portrait
*Saturday Evening Post,
February 13, 1960*

▶ The **sketches** show his alternative ideas for the self-portrait.

▶ The eagle and badge hint at his pride in being American.

▶ All his painting tools are included – an easel, palette, paints, and brushes.

▶ The open art book refers to Rockwell's huge library of art books. Coca Cola was his favourite drink.

◀ The helmet hints at a sense of grandeur about his work. But it is a joke, as this is, in fact, a French fireman's helmet.

◀ Self-portraits by artists Rockwell admires: Dürer, Rembrandt, Picasso and Van Gogh.

◀ Rockwell uses a **mahlstick,** as artists used to do, to keep his hand steady when painting details.

◀ Rockwell always signed his pictures. This signature on the **canvas** doubles as the one for the whole picture.

◀ The smoke is a reminder of the fire which destroyed his **studio** in 1943.

Me and my self-portrait

Norman Rockwell was an American **illustrator** who lived from 1894 to 1978. This self-portrait was used on the cover of a magazine that featured an article about Rockwell's life as an artist.

It's not surprising that he chose to picture himself at work in his studio. More unusually, he actually shows us three self-portraits: Rockwell as he 'really' is, seen head-to-toe from the back, peering into a mirror; his mirror image; and the **glamorized** self-portrait on the **easel**.

Use the clues in Rockwell's self-portrait to answer these questions.

- Was Rockwell tidy or messy?
- Was he sloppy or fussy about what he wore?
- Did he have good eyesight?
- Do you think Rockwell had a sense of humour?

❑ Norman Rockwell
Triple Self-Portrait (detail)

❑ Norman Rockwell
Triple Self-Portrait (detail)

The artist at work

Rockwell's picture shows exactly the way he worked:

- using art books for **reference**
- making pencil sketches
- using a mirror to study his face
- drawing an enlarged version of his head and shoulders on canvas
- squeezing blobs of **oil paints** on to a **palette**
- using a different brush for each colour.

Look at me

This self-portrait also shows the different ways artists can present themselves in images.

Rockwell painted his reflection to show an elderly, weedy, short-sighted person; not at all like the self-portrait drawn on the canvas.

How many differences can you spot?

Looking at self-portraits

Rembrandt and Van Gogh were both Dutch artists, who painted more pictures of themselves than any other painters did.

What a face!

Rembrandt used himself as a model to practise drawing facial expressions that portray different feelings, such as fear, worry, desperation, alarm, concern or amusement. In these self-portraits (like the one on the right), he focused only on his face. In other self-portraits, Rembrandt dressed up as a prince, a beggar, a soldier and a sultan.

A life in a face

Throughout his life, Rembrandt also created realistic self-portraits. Together, they tell the story of his life, from a happy and confident young man to an old and much sadder one.

❏ Rembrandt
Self-Portrait with Open Mouth and Eyes Wide Open, *1630*
This picture is an etching. An etching is made by drawing with a sharp, steel tool in a waxy layer melted on to a metal plate. The plate is dipped into acid, which bites into the lines of the metal exposed by the drawing. The wax is then cleaned off. Then the grooved plate is inked and paper pressed on to it to make prints.

• What feeling do you think Rembrandt is trying to express?

• How has he achieved this? Clue: look at the shape, size and position of his eyes and mouth.

This is how I feel

Van Gogh used particular colours and brushmarks to express how he felt inside, instead of just trying to copy his appearance exactly.

Cold colours

Van Gogh painted this self-portrait after he had been ill. He chose pale, icy colours both for his clothes and the background. There are cold tinges of green on his downturned lips and sunken cheeks, and around his staring eyes.

Swirls and curls

His **pose** seems calm. However, the waves and spirals, swirling both in the background and on his jacket, suggest restlessness, confusion and perhaps despair.

❑ Vincent Van Gogh
Self-Portrait, *1889*
Van Gogh painted 22 self-portraits in the two years between 1888 and 1890.

Me and my pet

Artists who are fond of their pets may include them in their self-portraits

◀ Hogarth's black fur cap is pushed back to reveal a deep scar from a childhood accident. This emphasizes his toughness.

◀ The portrait rests on books by famous English writers – Milton, Shakespeare and Swift. Hogarth wants to show he is an heir to their tradition of depicting the drama and comedy of human life.

◀ The curved s-line on the palette, which Hogarth called 'the line of beauty and grace', indicates that he was concerned with beauty in his paintings.

❑ William Hogarth, **Portrait of the Painter and his Pug**, *1745*

Me and my pug

This self-portrait by William Hogarth, an eighteenth-century English artist, features his pet dog, a pug, called Trump.

However, the picture has been painted in a curious way. Trump is shown as if alive sitting in front of a **bust**-length portrait of Hogarth. This painting-within-a-painting is propped up on books beside a palette. Why might Hogarth have painted his self-portrait like this?

• What similarities can you see between Hogarth and his dog? Clue: consider the look in their eyes, and shape of their noses.

• Why did Hogarth include an empty palette in the picture?

• How would you describe Hogarth's character from his portrait?

• What word would you use to sum up the dog's character?

❑ William Hogarth
Portrait of the Painter and his Pug (detail)

My pug is me

It may be that the dog, as well as being a beloved pet, also represents aspects of Hogarth's own character. Trump is keen and alert, with his ears cocked, listening for strange sounds. Pugs are an English breed known to be tough, stubborn and ready to fight. Perhaps these are qualities that Hogarth wanted to be known for, as well.

I am an artist

Some self-portraits emphasize the belief artists have in their work and the importance they attach to the tools of their trade.

My paintbrush and palette

Stanley Spencer, a twentieth-century English painter, holds up his brush with a flourish, as if to announce his pride in being a painter. He also tips up his palette, pushing it towards us, to show off the colours he has mixed. It takes up almost the width of the picture.

❏ Stanley Spencer
**Self-Portrait
(Adelaide Road)**
1939
Spencer painted this picture in a small attic room, where he was living alone, away from his family and friends. Behind him, you can see his rumpled bedsheets.

Preparing to paint

Spencer specifically focuses on his eyes and his hand, the two key assets of a painter. He gazes intently sideways as if studying himself in a mirror. His dark eyes are magnified and framed by his large glasses. His hand is raised in readiness to paint.

Pastel portraits

Rosalba Carriera, who lived in the eighteenth century, popularized portraits done in pastels, a recent invention in her time. Pastels are made of powdered **pigment**, mixed with chalk, water and gum or oils, and pressed into stumpy sticks. They were speedier and cheaper to use than oil paints and sitters did not need to pose for as long. Carriera shows her pastels in this self-portrait to advertise her skills. She grips a pastel holder and shows other colours spilling on to the table. By including the portrait she has drawn of her sister, Carriera showed that she could create head studies as well as half-length portraits.

Popular pictures

Carriera was very successful. She did portraits of the kings of both France and Poland, and many of rich nobles. She was elected to the painting **Academy** in Paris, a rare honour for a woman at that time.

- How would you describe the clothes both painters are wearing?
- Why do you think they have chosen these clothes for their self-portraits?
- Which of the colours on Spencer's palette can you find elsewhere in his self-portrait?

❏ Rosalba Carriera
Self-Portrait with a Portrait of her Sister
1715
Carriera was Italian. She taught her sisters to paint. Giovanna, shown here, became her lifelong assistant and helped to promote her work.

I am an important person

Look how Dürer has carefully built up an **idealized** portrait of himself.

◀ Dürer looks directly out at the viewer with a bold gaze. This makes him appear strong and confident – the equal of anyone who looks at him.

◀ The view of the distant Alps is a reminder of Dürer's visit to Italy, where he had been to study the work of Italian painters.

◀ Dürer has painted his finely pleated linen shirt, with its golden-edged neckline, in great detail, showing off his superb painting skills.

◀ His clasped, gloved hands suggest that he is above **manual** work.

❑ Albrecht Dürer,
Self-Portrait
1498

Artists may use self-portraits to promote themselves, just as Dürer has done here, as people of great importance.

Artisans and artists

Dürer lived at a time when painters in his country, Germany, were looked down on as **artisans**, working with their hands, rather than their minds.

After training as a **goldsmith** with his father and in several painters' **workshops**, Dürer travelled to Italy. He discovered how much Italian artists knew about literature, mathematics and geometry. He was impressed by how much people admired and respected the poetic imagination of these artists.

- How has Dürer shown that he was a skilful painter?
- Do you think that Dürer was proud of his looks?
- How would you describe Dürer's character?

❏ Albrecht Dürer
Self-Portrait (detail)

A fine gentleman

Dürer was determined to become not only an important artist, but also a scholar and a gentleman. He bought a big house, studied Latin and mathematics and wrote several books. In this self-portrait, his expensive clothes show that he would like to be considered elegant, fashionable and important. This detail of his hair shows that his painting was painstaking and meticulous.

❏ Albrecht Dürer
Self-Portrait
(detail)

An artist's signature

Dürer added an **inscription**, in Latin, to his self-portrait. It reads: '1498. I have thus painted myself. I was 26 years old. Albrecht Dürer.' He has also included his **monogram** (the interwoven initials, A and D), which later became the signature for many of his other works.

Me and my country

Some artists are very fond and proud of the country they come from, or of the place where they live. In their self-portraits, these artists may include details and **symbols**, and use particular colours, to identify or suggest a specific place.

Frida Kahlo, the Mexican

Frida Kahlo, who lived from 1907 to 1954, was deeply proud of being Mexican. She often wore traditional costumes and beads, and wove flowers and bright ribbons into her hair. She decorated her home with Mexican **folk art**, including paper cut-outs and flowers, holy pictures, masks, toys and painted furniture. She used many folk art **motifs** in her work.

Painted on glass and metal

Frida painted this self-portrait on glass, to look like her reflection in a mirror. She decorated the surrounding metal frame as well. She was inspired by Mexican folk artists who punched and painted vivid designs on tin objects.

❏ Frida Kahlo
The Frame: Self-Portrait
about 1938
This painting was shown at a Mexican exhibition in Paris in 1938. It was the first painting by a Mexican artist ever bought by the Louvre Museum in France.

Rousseau, the Frenchman

Rousseau has painted himself, larger than life, on a quay by the River Seine, which runs through Paris. The row of barrels, the ship with its flags and the toll house on the quayside are reminders that he had once been a **customs** officer. He holds a paintbrush and palette to show that he is now an artist. He has written his and his wives' names on the palette.

The tall Eiffel Tower behind the ship was completed only the year before this painting was made. The tower was the symbol of a huge exhibition in Paris, celebrating the 100th anniversary of the **French Revolution**.

❏ Henri Rousseau
Self-Portrait, from L'île Saint-Louis
1890
Some of Rousseau's pictures, like this one, show the world he saw around him. He is also famous for his exotic, dream-like scenes, often set in jungles.

Look for clues that tell you about where these two artists lived.

• Compare the strength of the colours. Which artist lived in a hot place?

• What things has Rousseau included to identify both the city and country where he lived?

Me and my world

☐ Marc Chagall
**Self-Portrait with
Seven Fingers**
1912-13

Artists can conjure up a whole world, that shows not only the setting where they work, but also gives a glimpse into their vivid imagination.

A studio in Paris

Marc Chagall (1887-1985) was a Jewish Russian artist who lived in France. Here, he shows himself hard at work in his Paris studio. You can tell he is in Paris, because the Eiffel Tower, the city's most famous landmark, is visible through his window. It is brilliantly lit up against the night sky – so too is a person floating down with a parachute. However, Chagall has turned his back on these spectacular sights of the city.

Done from memory

Instead, his mind is still full of dreams and memories of his childhood village, Jewish legends and Russian folk tales. His self-portrait clearly shows how these inspired his paintings. Notice his thought bubble above the easel, showing houses around a church, similar to the church in the painting on the easel. The picture on the easel is one that he also actually painted. It is called *To Russia, to the asses, and to the others'*.

A dream-like picture

The farmyard scene he is painting is very dream-like. A headless milkmaid floats in a night sky, spilling milk from her bucket, whilst her bright red cow stands on a roof.

Many viewpoints

Chagall was influenced by a group of painters called Cubists, who painted scenes from several points of view at once, using strong **geometrical** shapes. Notice the sharp angles on the artist's face, clothes and leg. He has also tilted the floor at a very steep angle to push the room out towards us.

Seven fingers

No one knows exactly why Chagall painted himself with seven fingers. Seven might have been his lucky number: he was born on the seventh day of the seventh month of the seventh year. Alternatively, it might refer to a **Yiddish** expression 'to do it with seven fingers', which means to do something well and very speedily.

- How would you describe the way that Chagall is dressed? Why might he have shown himself like this?
- How would you describe the way that Chagall uses colour?

Me and my interests

❏ Peter Blake, **The Toy Shop**, *1962*

You might wonder how a reconstruction of an old-fashioned toy shop could possibly be a self-portrait. Peter Blake, a contemporary British artist, chose the things in it very carefully to reflect his own interests, and to remind him of some of the toys, games and entertainments he enjoyed as a child.

A wondrous window display

Take a close look at the contents of the shop window. You will find all sorts of toys and models, comics, games, badges, jigsaws, magic tricks, masks, postcards and flags. There are also postcards of Elvis Presley, (the famous American rock and roll star), Popeye (a TV cartoon character), and models of cartoon characters from Disney films.

What a collection!

Peter Blake is a keen collector. He partly designed this work as his own museum: a safe place to store small, precious objects. The colourful, crowded arrangement is also a way of showing his excitement, as a child, of gazing into the busy window of an old-fashioned toy shop.

Child-sized

Although this work has been made to look like a real shop front, the door, the window and the wall are, in fact, child-sized. The door was originally part of a cupboard. The shop front is painted in the bright colours often used for children's toys. The area behind the window is very shallow, so that the work can hang on the wall, like a painting.

❏ Peter Blake
The Toy Shop (detail)

• What shows Blake's interest in painting?
• What shows that he liked playing practical jokes?
• What clues display the artist's love of fairgrounds and circuses?
• What sort of games did Blake enjoy playing?
• How does Blake express his nationality?
• Find six different sorts of toys.

Myself as a chair

Could you paint a portrait of yourself as a chair? Van Gogh, the Dutch nineteenth-century painter, did. He painted these two chairs to express how different he and his French painter friend, Paul Gauguin, were.

Gauguin's visit

Van Gogh invited Gauguin to stay with him in Arles, in the south of France. He hoped to start an artists' group, but the painters kept arguing. After only two months, Gauguin left.

Van Gogh's chair

This is a daytime picture. Van Gogh's chair reflects the way he lived, painting what he saw around him. It is a plain, sturdy chair with a straw seat, standing on a hard, tiled floor. The pipe and tobacco on it show one of his simple pleasures. The bulbs sprouting in the box suggest that nature inspired Van Gogh's work.

❑ Vincent van Gogh
The Chair and the Pipe
before *1889*
Do you think Van Gogh hung these pictures together with the chairs facing one another like this, as a sign of friendship and conversation, or back to back as a sign of disagreement and rejection?

• How many differences can you spot between the two chairs?

20

□ Vincent van Gogh
Gauguin's Chair
1888

• Compare the colour and textures
in the two rooms. How do the colours
make you feel?

Gauguin's chair

This is a night-time picture. Gauguin believed that paintings should show ideas that come from the artist's imagination or from books. That is why Van Gogh painted Gauguin's chair as a comfortable gentleman's chair with two books on it. The chair stands on a soft carpet in a wallpapered room. The room colours are dark and rich, similar to those Gauguin used in his paintings. The lit gas lamp and candle both suggest Gauguin's night-time reading and reveries.

Dabs and dashes

Van Gogh painted quickly and energetically, using thick dabs and dashes of paint. You can see the direction of each raised, paint-loaded brush stroke. This way of painting is called *impasto*.

Me and my workplace

Sometimes, the setting of a self-portrait can reveal a great deal about an artist.

The king's painter

Pierre Mignard, a French artist working in the seventeenth century, painted this self-portrait when he became King Louis XIV's First Painter and director of the Royal Academy of Painting and Sculpture. He succeeded his bitter, life-long rival, Charles Le Brun. Le Brun had been more successful in gaining the king's favour and getting important **commissions** for portraits and decorations for palaces and churches. Mignard had been very jealous and resentful of Le Brun.

A sumptuous room

When Mignard finally took over Le Brun's position, he wanted to prove that he was just as good an artist. Every detail in this self-portrait was deliberately included to bolster Mignard's view of his abilities and achievements. He showed himself at work in a grand room in the king's palace. Notice the pillars, the heavy curtains with hanging tassels, the grand velvet chair and the matching velvet tablecloth.

- Think of a word to describe the atmosphere of Mignard's room.
- What clues does the artist give about the kind of work he does?
- What view does he have of his role as an artist?

Looking good

Although Mignard was almost eighty when he painted this picture, he shows himself looking far younger. He is dressed in an expensive dressing gown, and wears a wig, like other gentlemen of his time.

An artist's tools

Mignard portrays himself hard at work, sketching from his imagination. In the left-hand corner of the picture, he included a **still life** of his painting equipment: a paint palette, a variety of brushes, a pair of compasses, a rolled-up canvas, a sketchbook and a mahlstick. The sculpted bust behind is a portrait of Catherine, his favourite child and only daughter, who was a model for several of his pictures.

◀ Mignard displayed his designs for a church dome, commissioned by the Queen of France. He was very proud of this work.

◀ He included small statues of two goddesses, Venus and Diana, to indicate his wide knowledge of ancient mythology.

◀ This drawing of Trajan's column, in Rome, may refer to Mignard's nickname, 'The Roman', as he lived in Italy for many years.

❑ Pierre Mignard
Self-Portrait
about *1690*

A photo of me

Photography is another medium that artists can use for making self-portraits, sometimes with surprising results.

An automatic self-portrait

Before he could afford a camera of his own, Andy Warhol, a twentieth-century American artist, experimented with cheap photobooth photos to create a series of self-portraits. He liked the fact that photobooths were automatic and anonymous, and that they produced multiple images in a sequence, like these.

Machine made

Warhol was intrigued by the sameness of machine-made goods. Notice how these images all have the same background and that the **flash** produces the same amount of contrast between light and shade.

❏ Andy Warhol
Source Material, Photobooth pictures *n.d.*
Sometimes, Warhol directed models in a photo-booth, telling them how to position their head or neck, or what expressions to make. He later used the photographs as a basis for printed portraits.

Two-faced me

By contrast, Wanda Wulz's self-portrait was created by using a photographic trick. She put a **negative** of a cat's face on top of a negative of her own face. When printed together, they merged into a single face.

In hiding

Photographic images are often accepted as revealing the truth. However, as both these self-portraits show, people can also hide themselves in a photograph. Whichever way he turns, Warhol's dark sunglasses and deadpan expression give away few clues about him, and Wulz is completely fused with the cat.

- What impression of Warhol's character can you gain from his photos?
- What effect do Warhol's sunglasses have on his image?
- Which parts of Wulz's picture are the cat's face and which are her own?

❑ Wanda Wulz, **Me + Cat**, *1932*
Wulz was trained by her father, who ran a photographic studio, founded by her grandfather, in 1868, in Trieste, Italy. She took over the studio, at the age of 25, when her father died, and ran it herself for over 50 years.

A sculptural self-portrait

Sculptors can create self-portraits in metal, clay, wood or stone.

In the guise of a god

Eduardo Paolozzi, who was born in 1924, created his larger than life self-portrait in the **guise** of Hephaestos, the ancient Greek blacksmith god of fire and patron of craftsmen. Hephaestos was said to have made metal weapons and magic armour for the gods; shaped Pandora, the first woman, from clay; and created moving metal figures that were almost human. As a sculptor, also working with metal and creating robot-like figures, Paolozzi felt a strong connection with Hephaestos, and combined an image of this mythical god with his own.

Mechanic with imagination

Paolozzi trained as a mechanic before becoming a sculptor. He worried that in this machine and computer age, people were losing their ability to make things and did not appreciate the past, the imagination and spiritual things.

- Does Paolozzi look young or old?
- Does he look strong or weak?
- What do you think he is holding in his hands?
- Hephaestos was lame. How has Paolozzi shown this?

Machine men

Before making his self-portrait, Paolozzi had constructed a series of heads and figures that were half-man, half-machine, to express the way he felt. Many of them were made from junk, then **cast** in metal.

Constructed in pieces

Paolozzi deliberately wanted to show that his self-portrait was constructed from different pieces and that they did not all fit. Notice how his head had been modelled, sliced apart and the parts then reassembled to make a new, almost robotic portrait. This sculpture stands in a specially made niche outside an office block in London, England.

About the artists

The symbols below show the size and shape of the works shown in this book, compared with an average-sized adult.

Peter BLAKE (pages 18-19)

(1932-) British
The Toy Shop, 1962
Mixed media, 156.8 x 194 x 34 cm
Tate Britain, London, UK

Other works

❑ *Self-Portrait in RAF Jacket,* about 1952-3
  Private Collection
❑ *Self-Portrait with Badges,* 1961
  Tate Britain, London, UK

Rosalba CARRIERA (page 11)

(1675-1757) Italian (Venice)
Self-Portrait with a Portrait of her Sister, 1715
Pastel on paper, 71 x 57 cm
Uffizi Gallery, Florence, Italy

Other self-portraits

❑ *Self-Portrait as Winter,* 1731
  Gemäldegalerie, Dresden, Germany
❑ *Self-Portrait,* 1744
  Royal Collection, Windsor, UK
❑ *Self-Portrait,* 1745
  Accademia, Venice, Italy

Marc CHAGALL (pages 16-17)

(1887-1985) French (born Russian)
Self-Portrait with Seven Fingers, 1912-13
Oil on canvas, 126 x 107 cm
Stedelijk Museum, Amsterdam, Netherlands

Other self-portraits

❑ *Self-Portrait with Brushes,* 1909
  Kunstsammlung Nordrhein-Westfalen,
  Düsseldorf, Germany
❑ *Self-Portrait,* 1914
  Kunstmuseum, Bern, Switzerland.
❑ *Self-Portrait,* 1914
  Philadelphia Museum of Art, Philadelphia, PA, USA

Albrecht DÜRER (pages 12-13)

(1471-1528) German
Self-Portrait, 1498
Oil on wood, 52 x 41 cm
Prado Museum, Madrid, Spain

Other self-portraits

❑ *Portrait of the Artist Holding a Thistle,* 1493
  Louvre, Paris, France
❑ *Self-Portrait with a Fur Coat,* 1500
  Alte Pinakothek, Munich, Germany

Vincent van GOGH (pages 7, 20-21)

(1853-90) Dutch
Self-Portrait, 1889
Oil on canvas, 65 x 54 cm
Musée d'Orsay, Paris, France

The Chair and the Pipe, before 1889
Oil on canvas, 92 x 73 cm
National Gallery, London, UK

Gauguin's Chair, 1888
Oil on canvas, 90.5 x 72 cm
Rijksmuseum Vincent van Gogh
Amsterdam, Holland

Other self-portraits

- *Self-Portrait with Grey Felt Hat*, 1887
  Rijksmuseum Vincent van Gogh,
  Amsterdam, Netherlands
- *Self-Portrait with a Straw Hat*, about 1888
  Metropolitan Museum of Art, New York, USA
- *Self-Portrait in front of an Easel*, 1888
  Rijksmuseum Vincent van Gogh,
  Amsterdam, Netherlands
- *Self-Portrait with Bandaged Ear*, 1889
  Courtauld Institute Galleries, London, UK

William HOGARTH (pages 8-9)

(1697-1746) English
Portrait of the Painter and his Pug, 1745
Oil on canvas, 90 x 69 cm
Tate Britain, London, UK

Another self-portrait

- *Self-Portrait (at an easel)* about 1757
  National Portrait Gallery, London, UK

Frida KAHLO (page 14)

(1907-54) Mexican
The Frame: Self-Portrait, about 1938
Oil on aluminium and glass, 29 x 22 cm
Musée Nationale d'Art Moderne, Paris, France

Other self-portraits

- *Frida and Diego Rivera,* 1931
  Albert M Bender Collection,
  San Francisco Museum of Modern Art, CA, USA
- *Self-Portrait (dedicated to Leon Trotsky)*, 1937
  National Museum of Women in the Arts,
  Washington DC, USA
- *Self-Portrait with Monkey*, 1938
  Allbright-Knox Art Gallery, Buffalo, New York, USA

Pierre MIGNARD (pages 22-23)

(1612-95) French
Self-Portrait, about 1690
Oil on canvas, 235 x 188cm
Louvre, Paris, France

Eduardo PAOLOZZI (pages 26-27)

(1924-) Scottish (of Italian parents)
The Artist as Hephaestos, 1987
Bronze, 264 cm high
34-36 High Holborn, London, UK

Other self-portraits

- *Sir Eduardo Luigi Paolozzi,* 1987
  National Portrait Gallery, London, UK

REMBRANDT (page 6)

(1606-69) Dutch
*Self-Portrait with Open Mouth and Eyes
Wide Open,* 1630
Etching, 51 x 46 cm
Rijksmuseum, Amsterdam, Netherlands

Other self-portraits

- *Self-Portrait in Oriental Costume,
  with a Dog,* 1631
  Musée du Petit Palais, Paris, France
- *Self-Portrait,* 1640
  The National Gallery, London, UK
- *Self-Portrait,* about 1668
  Kenwood House, Iveagh Bequest, London, UK

Norman ROCKWELL (pages 4-5)

(1894-1978) American
Triple Self-Portrait, 1960
Oil on canvas, 113.5 x 87.5 cm
Saturday Evening Post, February 13, 1960

Other self-portraits

❏ *Norman Rockwell Visits a Country Editor*, 1946
   National Press Club, Washington DC, USA
❏ *Rockwell and his Wife, Molly*, 1967
   Collection Norman Rockwell Museum, Stockbridge,
   MA, USA

Henri ROUSSEAU (page 15)

(1844-1910) French
Self-Portrait, from L'île Saint-Louis, 1890
Oil on canvas, 146 x 113 cm
Narodni Galerie, Prague, Czech Republic

Another self-portrait

❏ *Self-Portrait of the Artist with a Lamp*, 1903
   Musée Picasso, Paris, France

Stanley SPENCER (page 10)

(1891-1959) British
Self-Portrait (Adelaide Road), 1939
Oil on canvas 39.7 x 55.2 cm
Fitzwilliam Museum, Cambridge, UK

Other self-portraits

❏ *Self-Portrait*, 1914
   Tate Britain, London, UK
❏ *Self-Portrait*, 1936
   Stedelijk Museum, Amsterdam, Netherlands
❏ *Self-Portrait*, 1959
   Tate Britain, London, UK

Andy WARHOL (page 24)

(1928-87) American
Source Material, Photobooth pictures n.d.,
Gelatin silver print on photographic paper,
19.8 x 4 cm
The Andy Warhol Museum, Pittsburgh,
PA, USA

Other self-portraits

❏ *Self-Portrait with Skull*, 1978
   The Andy Warhol Museum, Pittsburgh, PA, USA
❏ *Self-Portraits (Polaroid photographs)*,1981-2
   The Andy Warhol Museum, Pittsburgh, PA, USA
❏ *Last Self-Portrait*, 1986
   Metropolitan Museum of Art, New York, USA

Wanda WULZ (page 25)

(1903-1984)
Me + Cat, 1932
Photomontage, 29.3 x 23.2 cm
Private collection

Glossary

Academy An official place, from the eighteenth century onwards, where artists were trained.

Artisan Someone skilled at a handcraft.

Bust A view of someone's head and shoulders.

Canvas A piece of coarse, stretched cloth on which artists often paint.

Cast Shape metal (or other material) by melting it and pouring it into a mould.

Commissions Orders and payments for making particular works of art.

Customs Money that governments charge when people bring things into a country.

Easel The stand on which artists rest their canvas for painting.

Flash Part of a camera that makes a burst of bright light, for taking photographs in poor light.

Folk art Traditional art made by ordinary people.

French Revolution The overthrow by the French people of the king and government in France, from 1789 to 1799.

Geometrical Mathematical shapes such as squares, circles or triangles.

Glamorized Made to seem better or more beautiful.

Goldsmith Someone who makes gold objects.

Guise Appearance or manner.

Idealized Made better than it really is.

Illustrator Someone who makes pictures for books, magazines or newspapers.

Inscription Words written on the surface of something – often carved on a piece of stone.

Mahlstick A stick with a padded ball at one end, used by a painter to support and steady the hand holding the paintbrush.

Manual Using one's hands.

Medium A material used by an artist, such as paint, pastels, photographs, stone, or metal.

Monogram Two or more interwoven letters, usually a person's initials.

Motifs Decorative designs.

Negative Photographic film showing light and shade, or colours, reversed from the original. Positive prints are made from negatives.

Oil paints Thick paints made by mixing ground pigments with oils.

Palette The wooden board on which artists lay out and mix their paints.

Pigment The colour in paint.

Pose To stay in a particular position for an artist to draw, paint or photograph.

Reference A source of information.

Sketches Quick drawings of what things look like, often done as a guide for a more detailed painting.

Still life A picture of a group of objects, such as flowers, food, utensils, tools or crockery.

Studio An artist's workplace.

Symbols Things that stand for something else.

Workshop The name for an artist's studio at the time when artists needed assistants to help prepare their paints.

Yiddish A language used by Jewish people from central and eastern Europe.

Index

Numbers in **bold** show page numbers of illustrations